Faces Adult Coloring Book

This Coloring book belongs to:

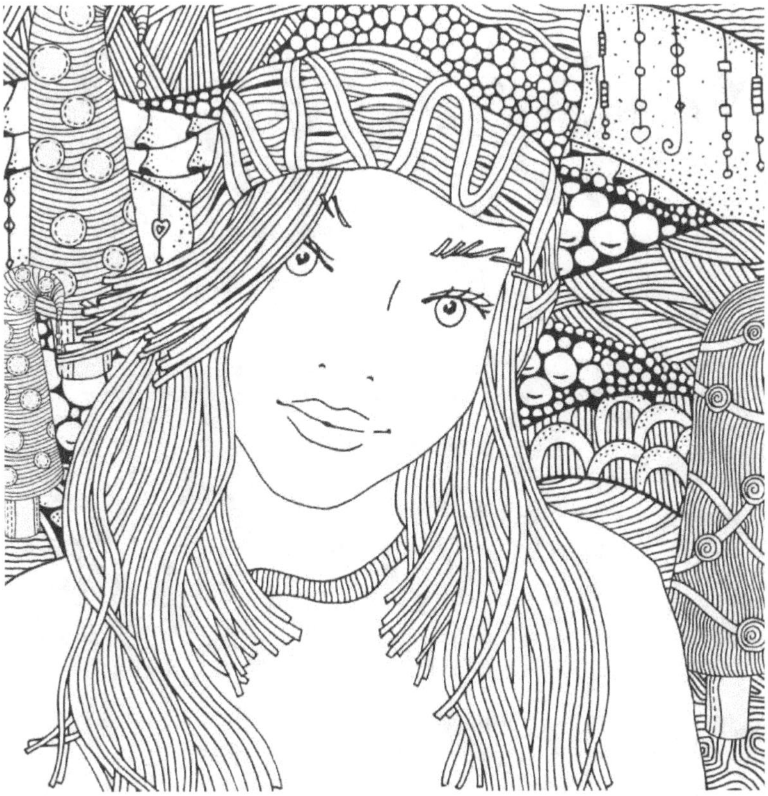

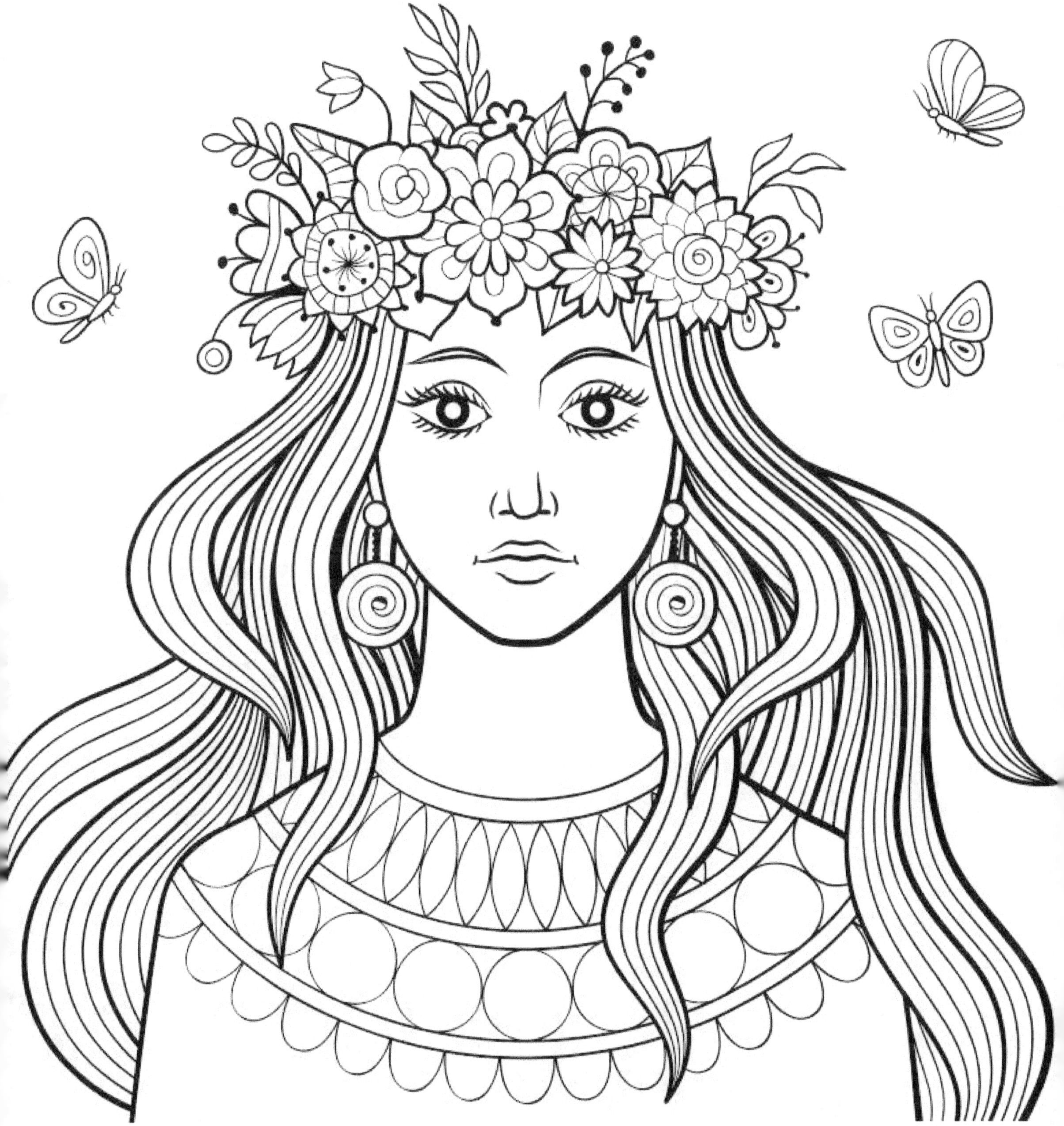

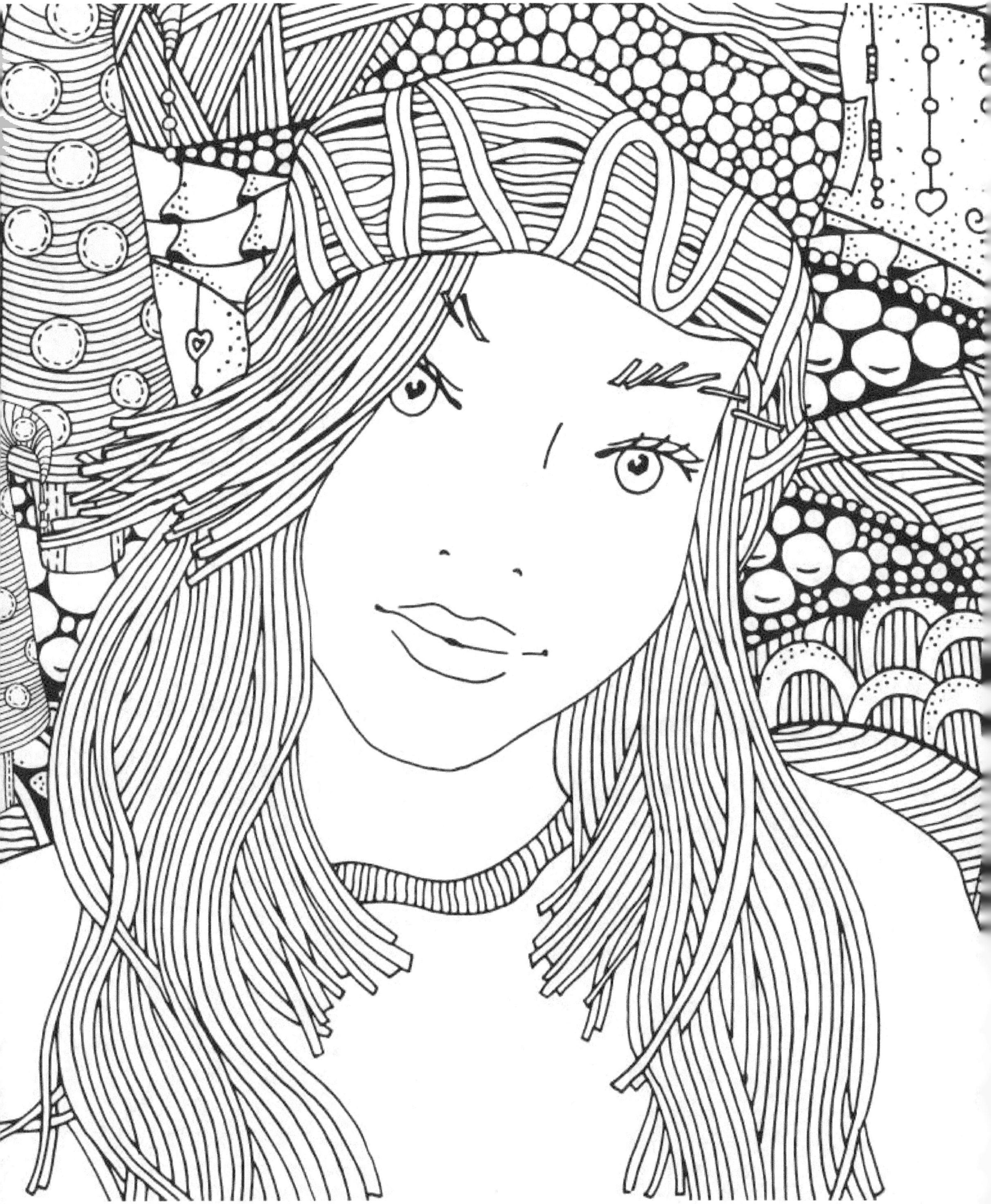

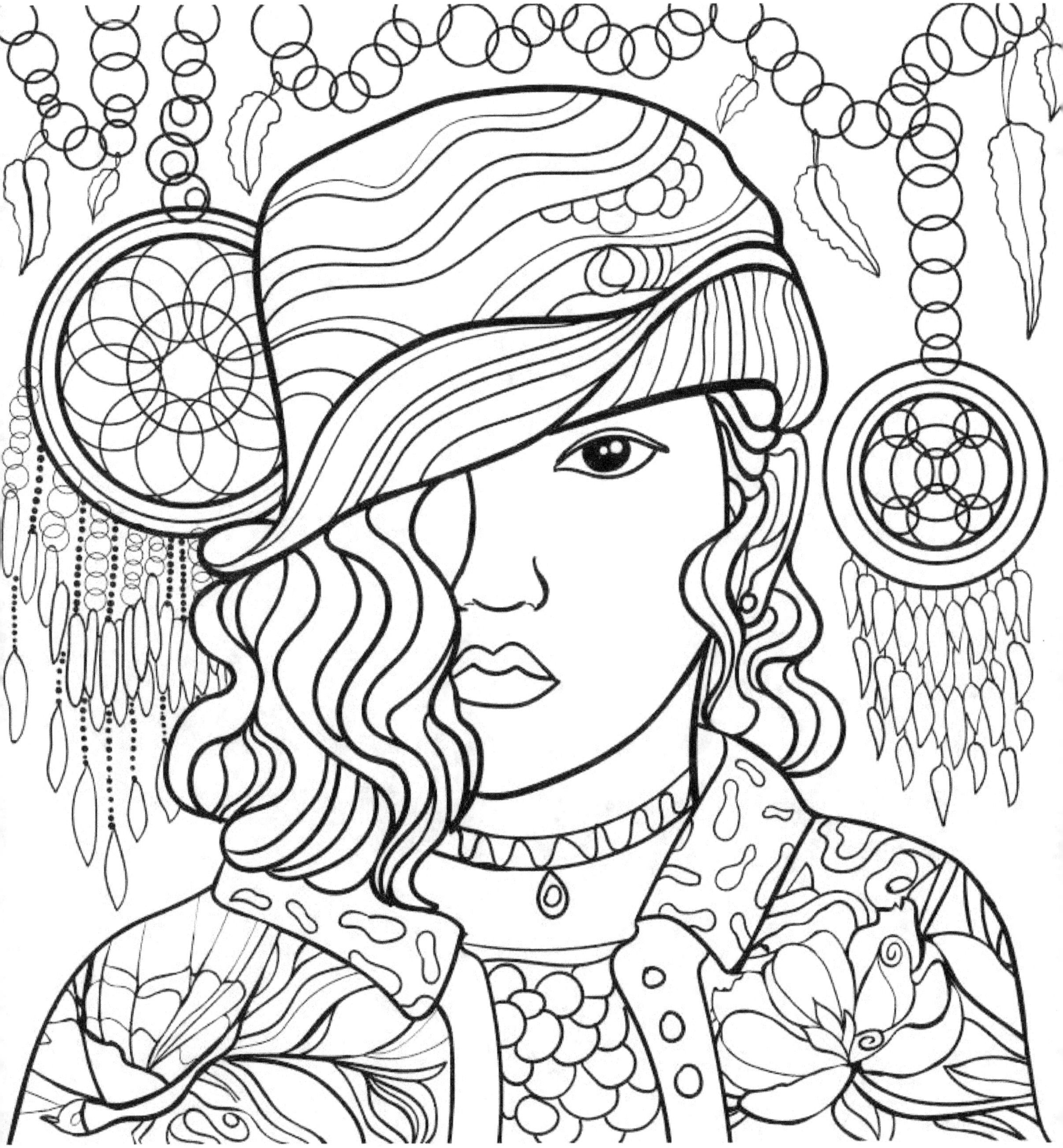

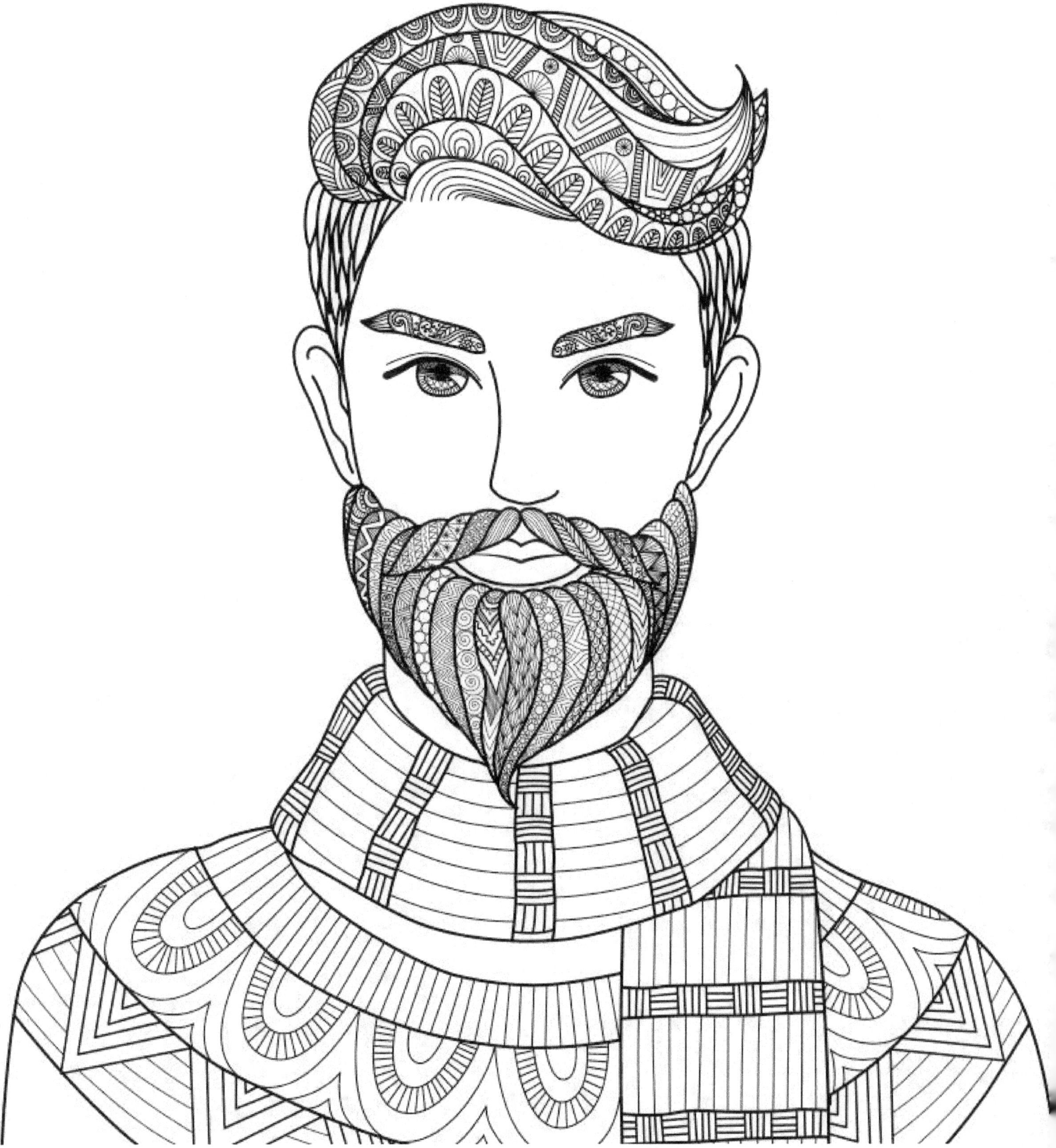

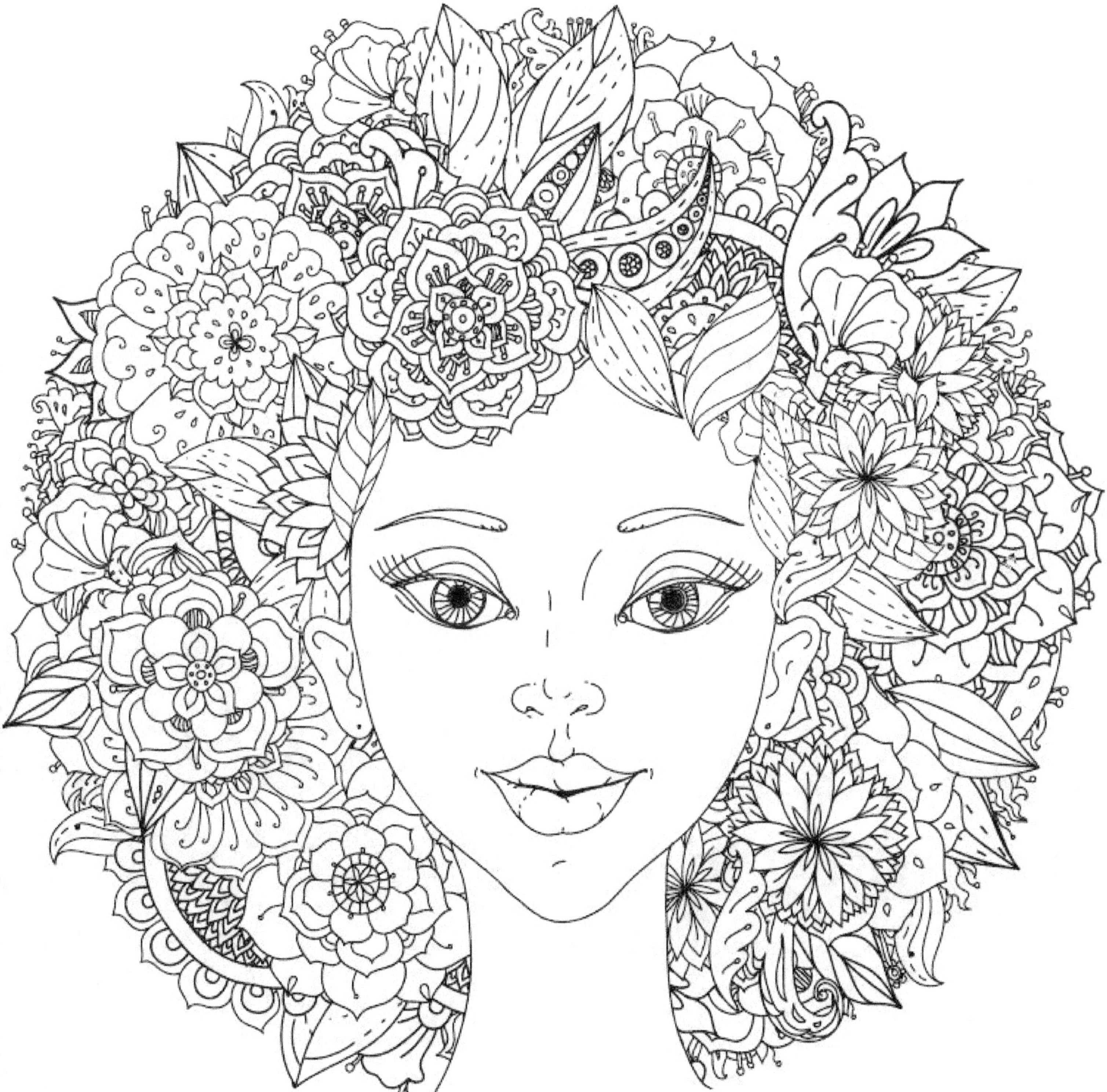

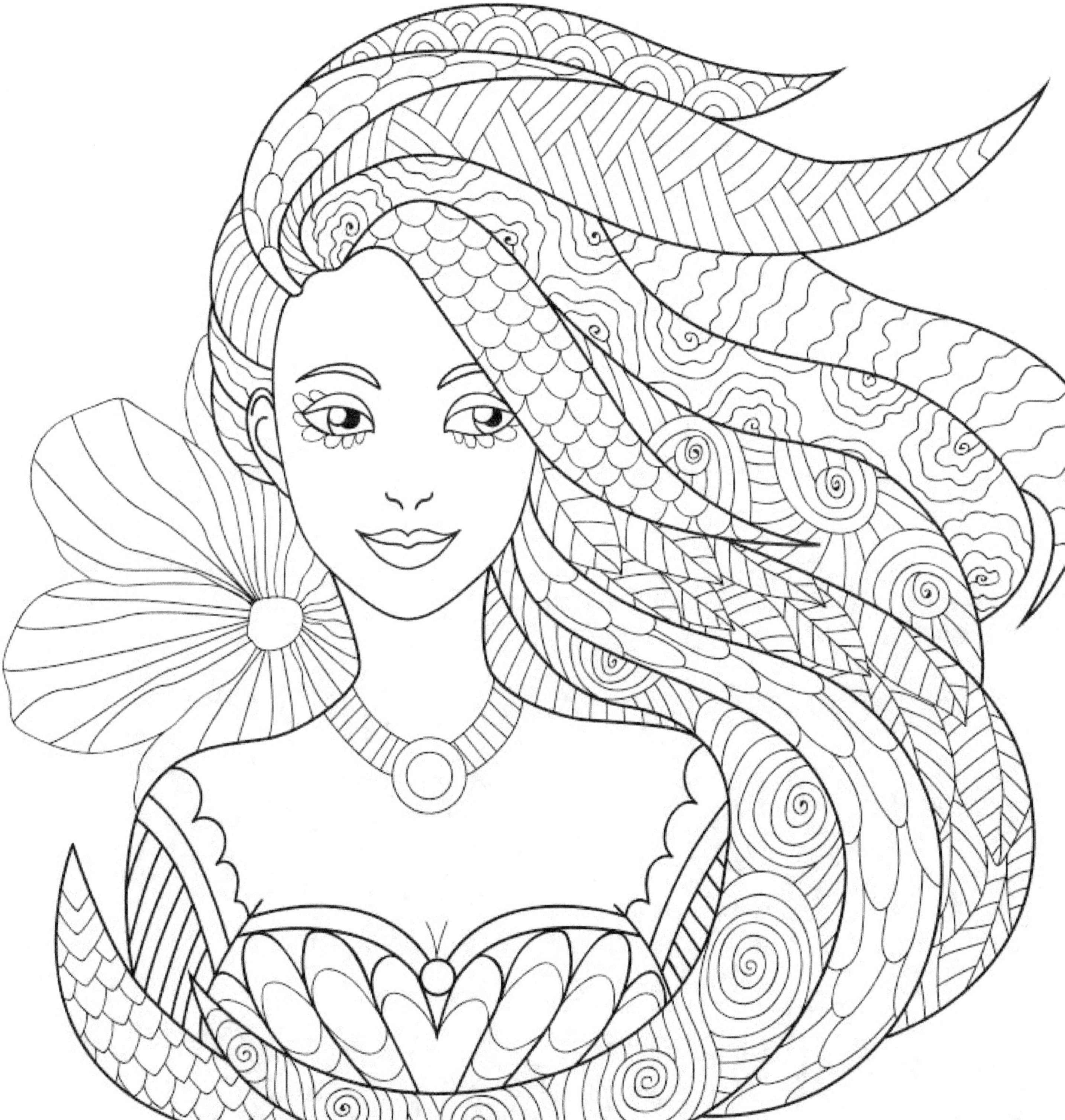

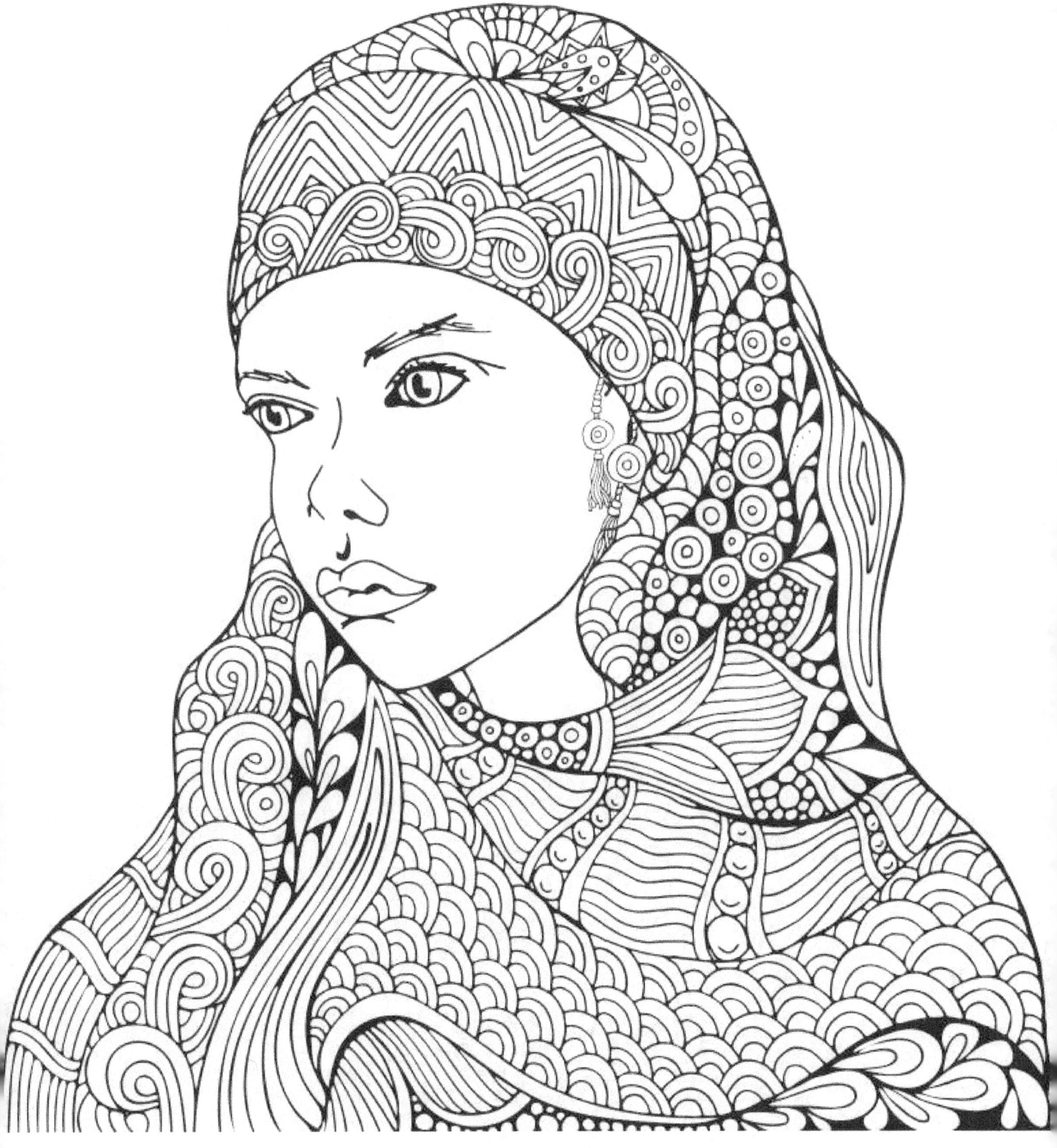

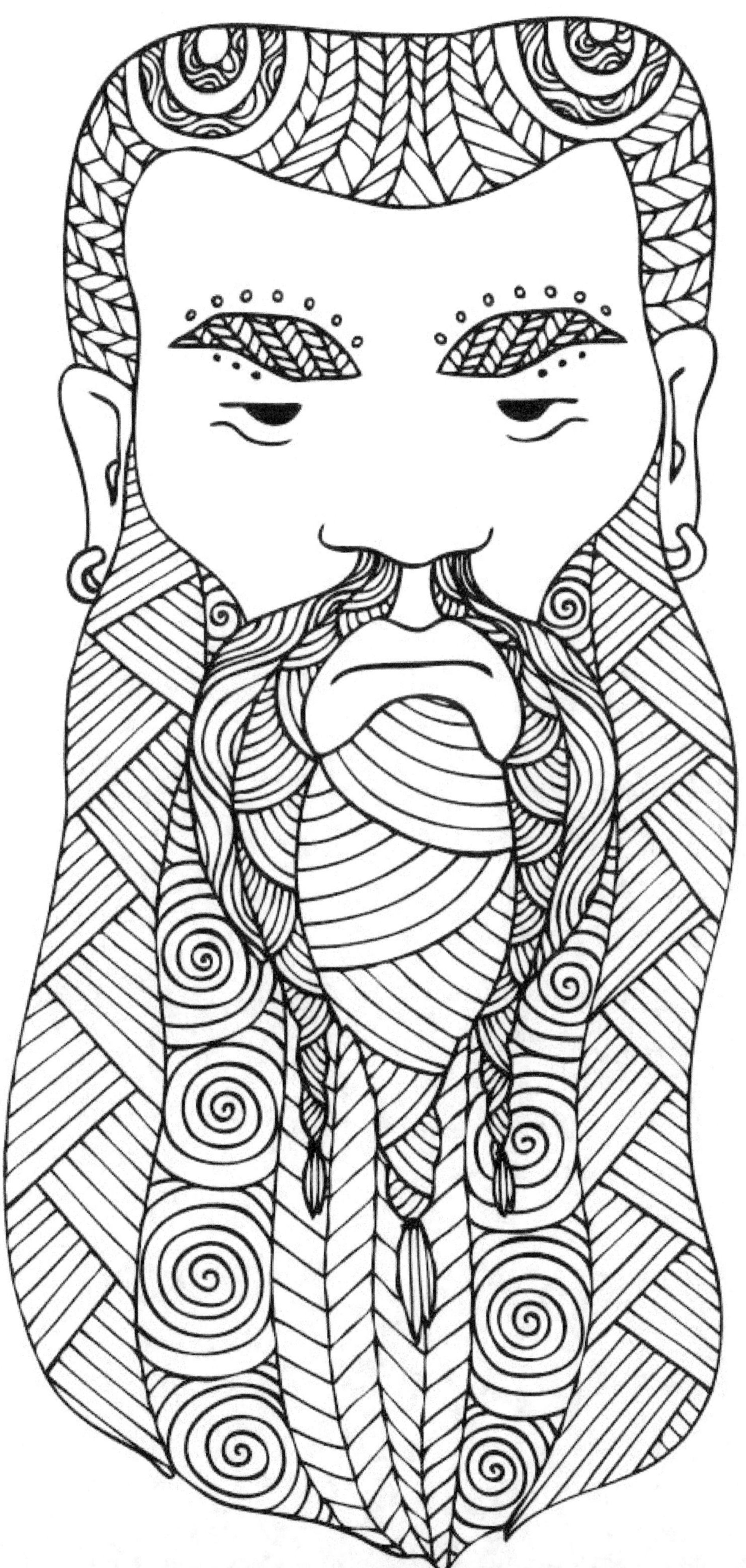

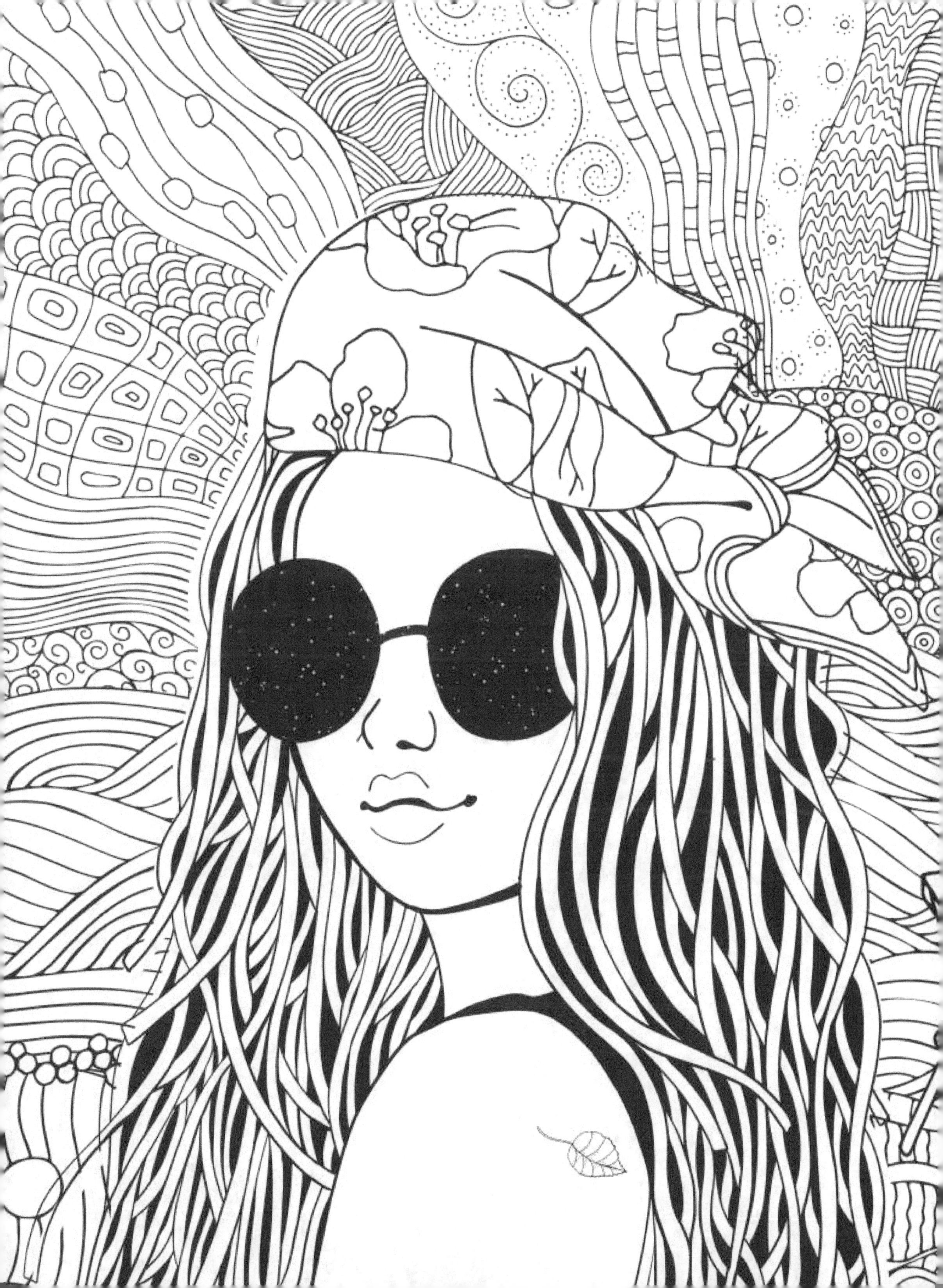

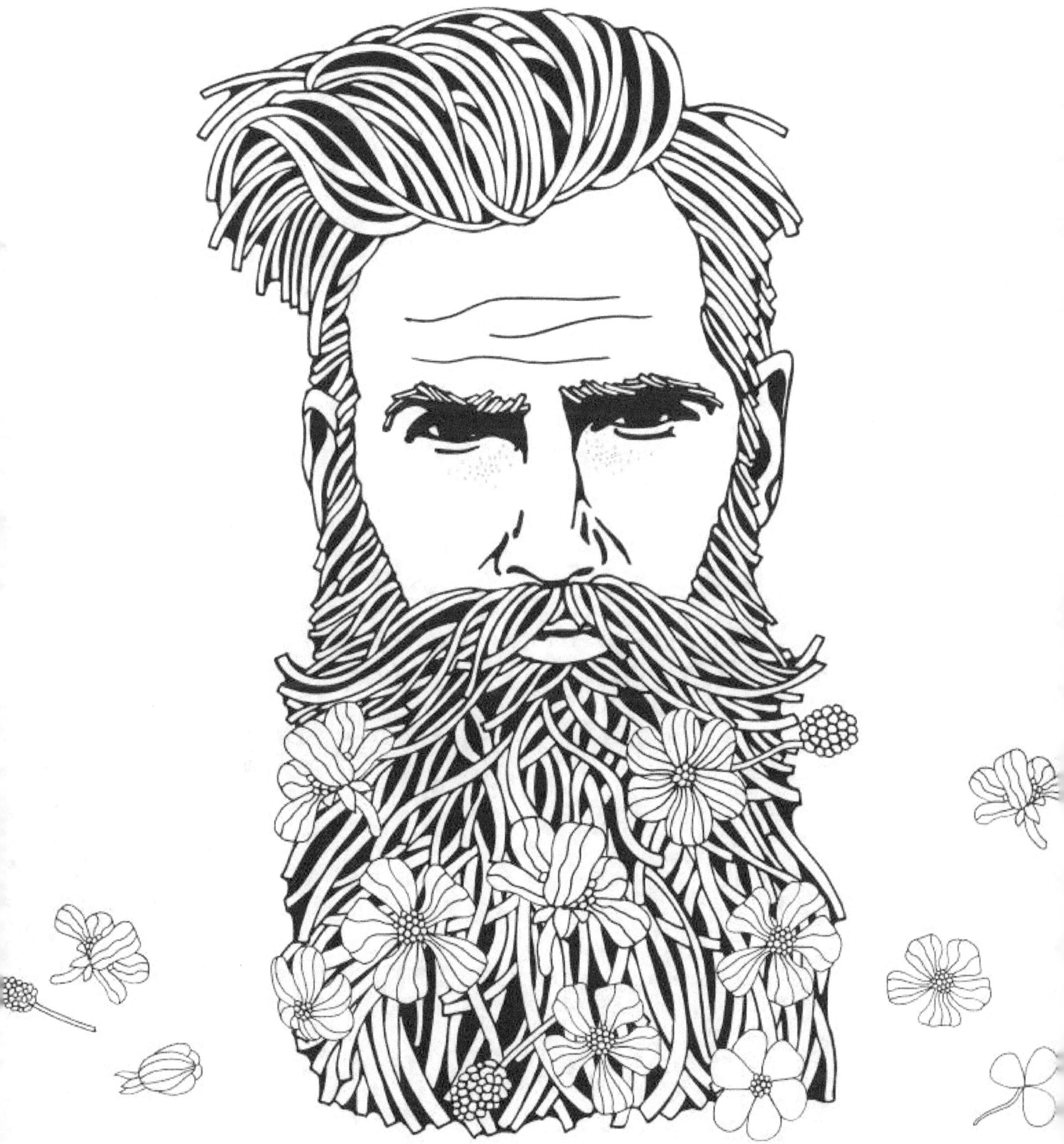

Surprise Bonus Beautiful Birds Coloring Pages to Enjoy.

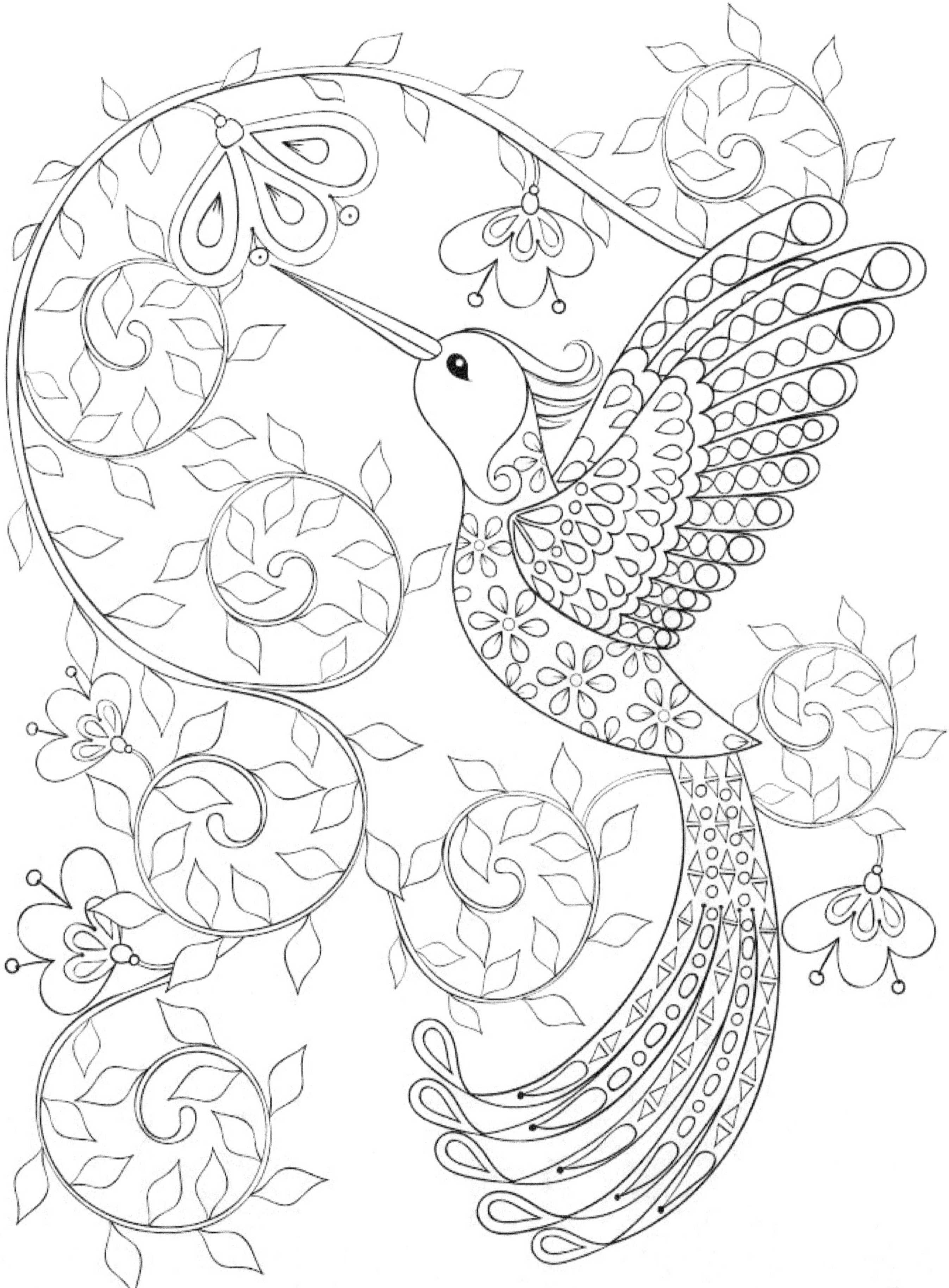

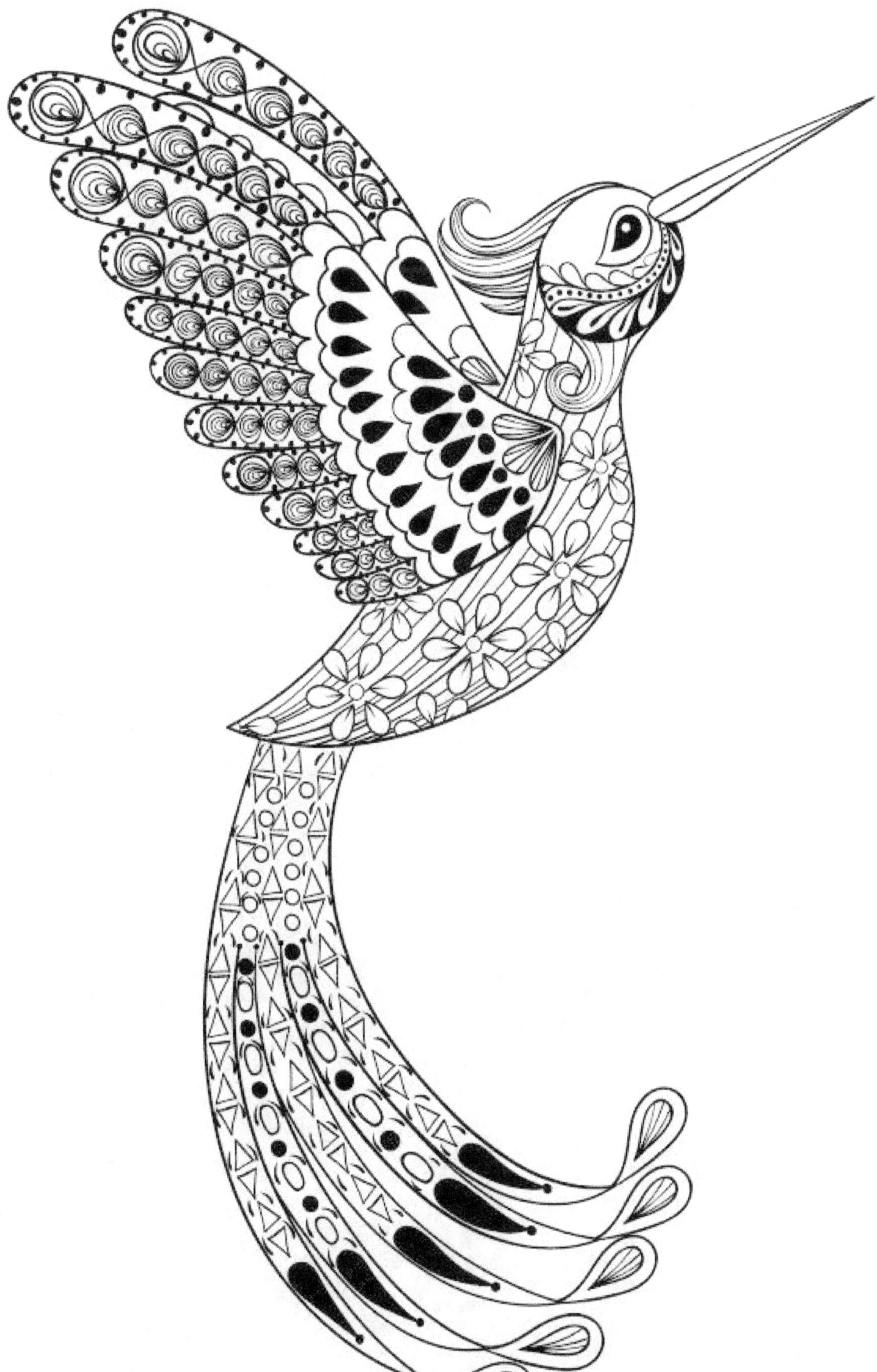

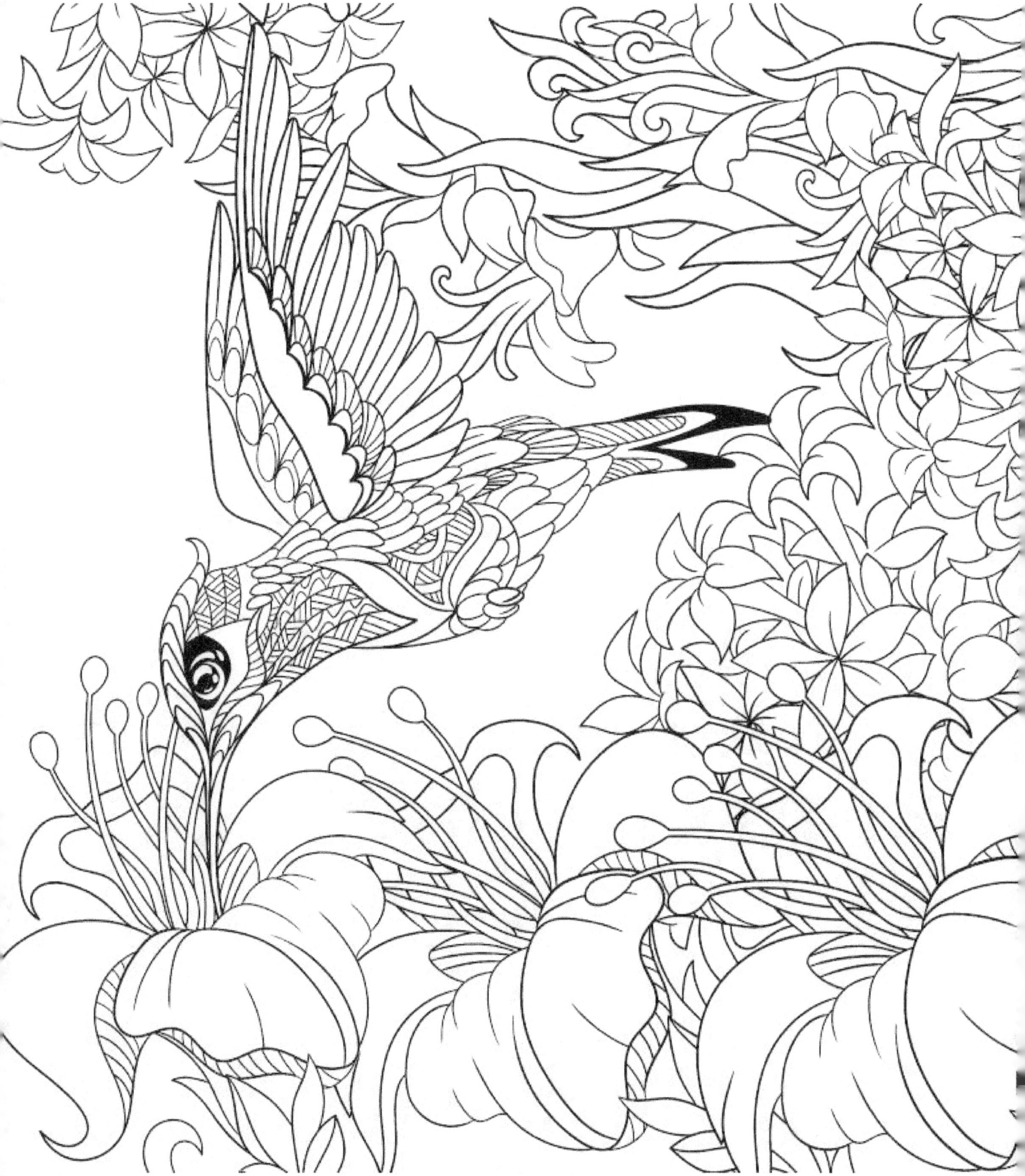

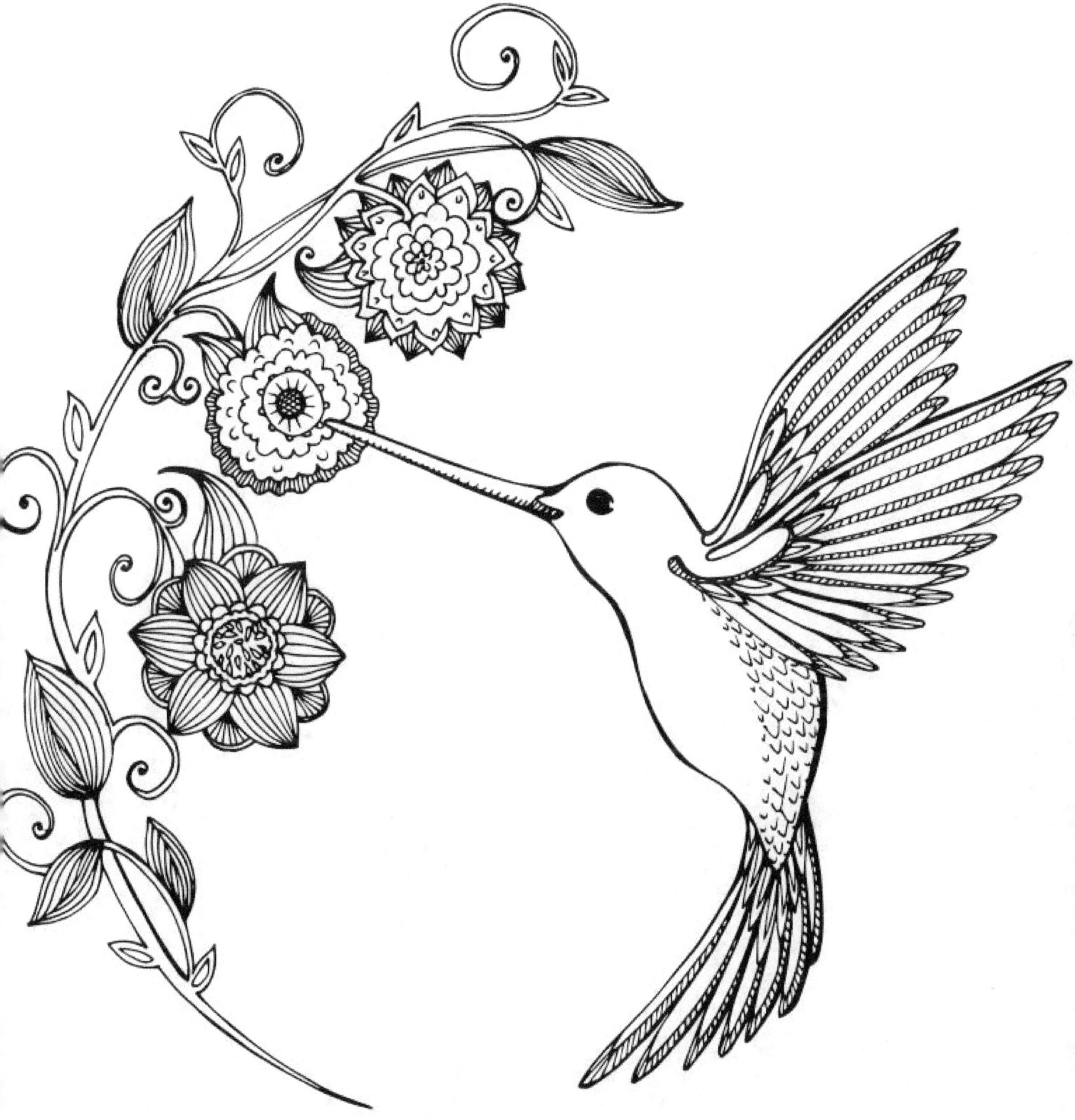

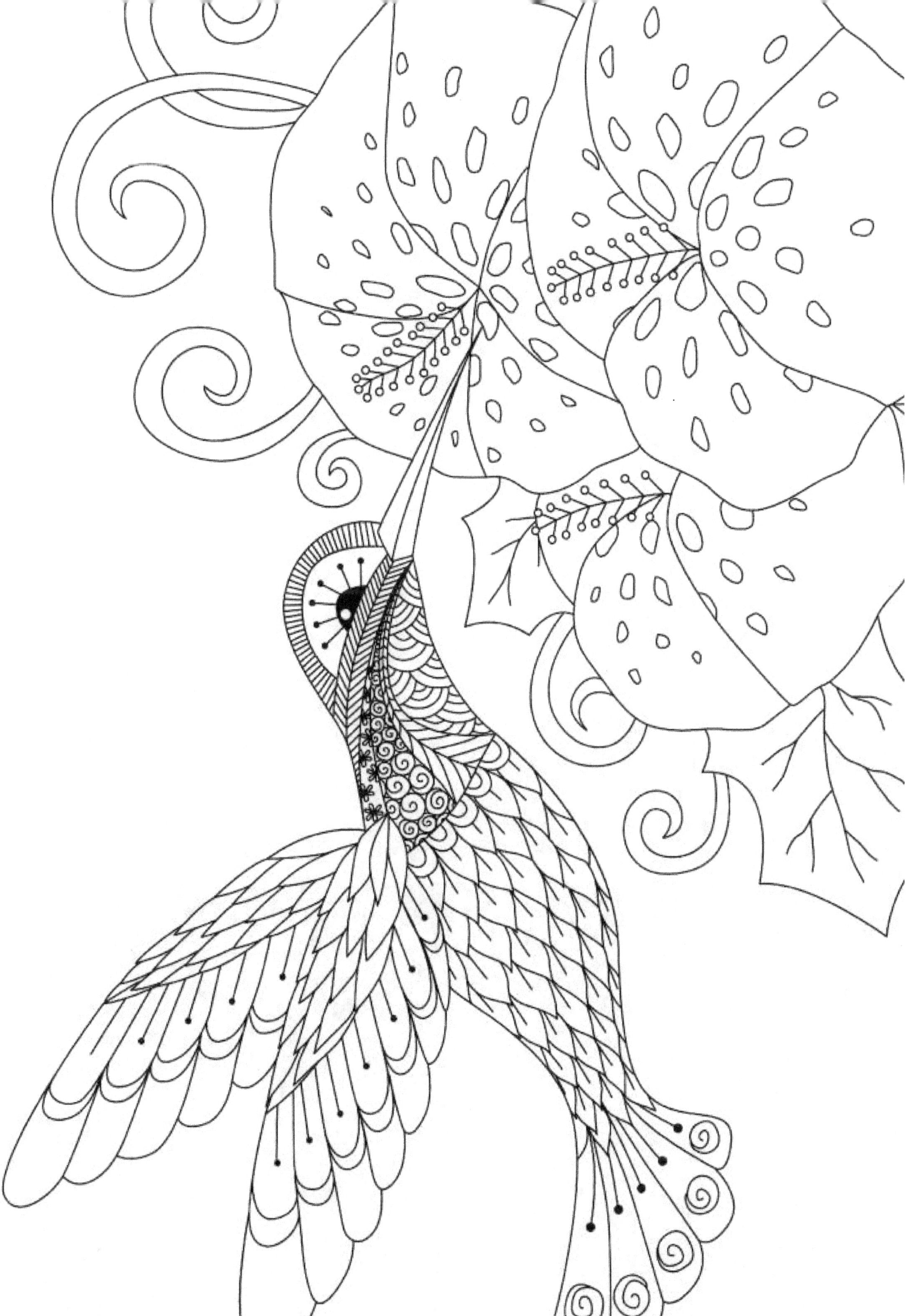

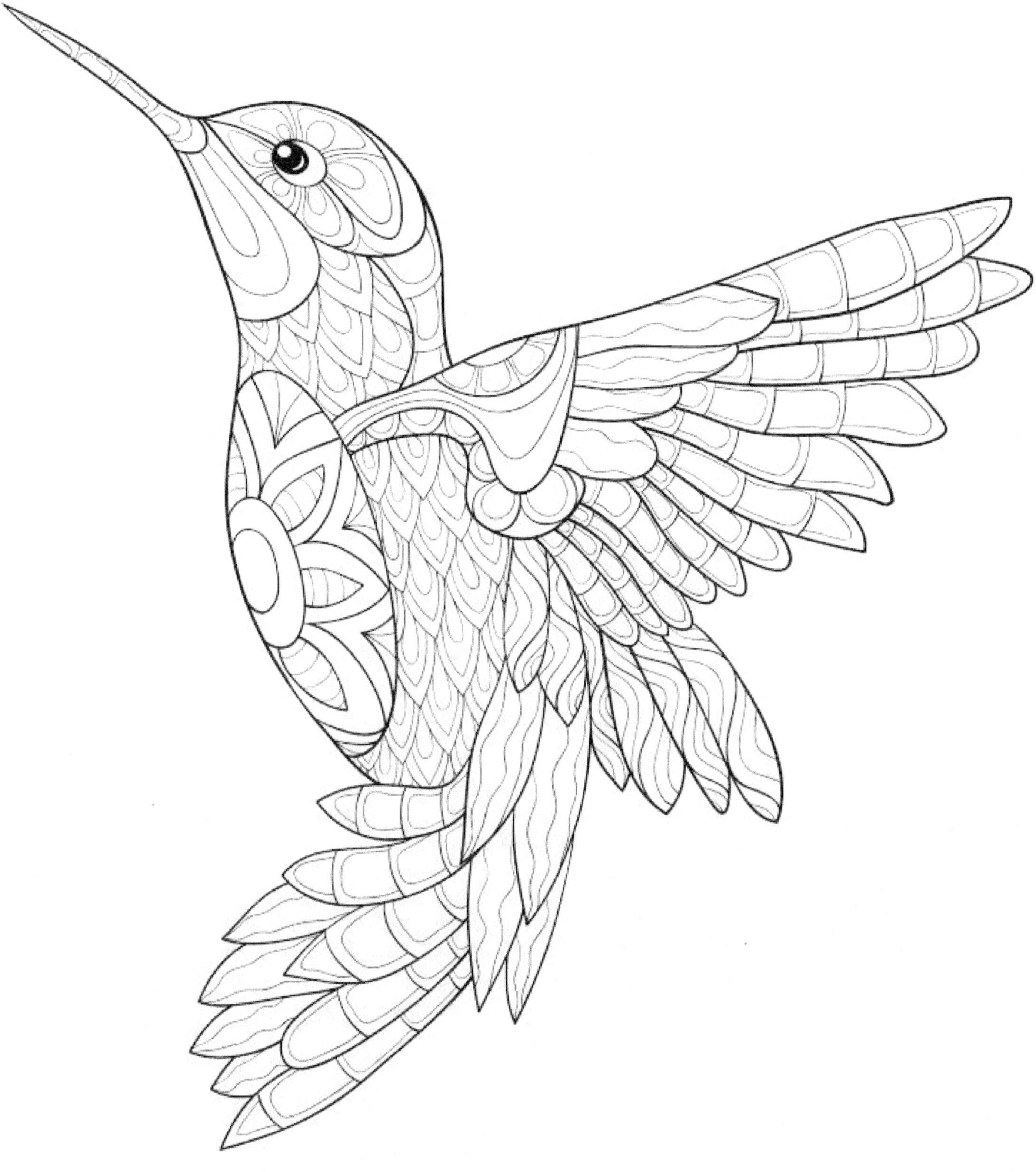

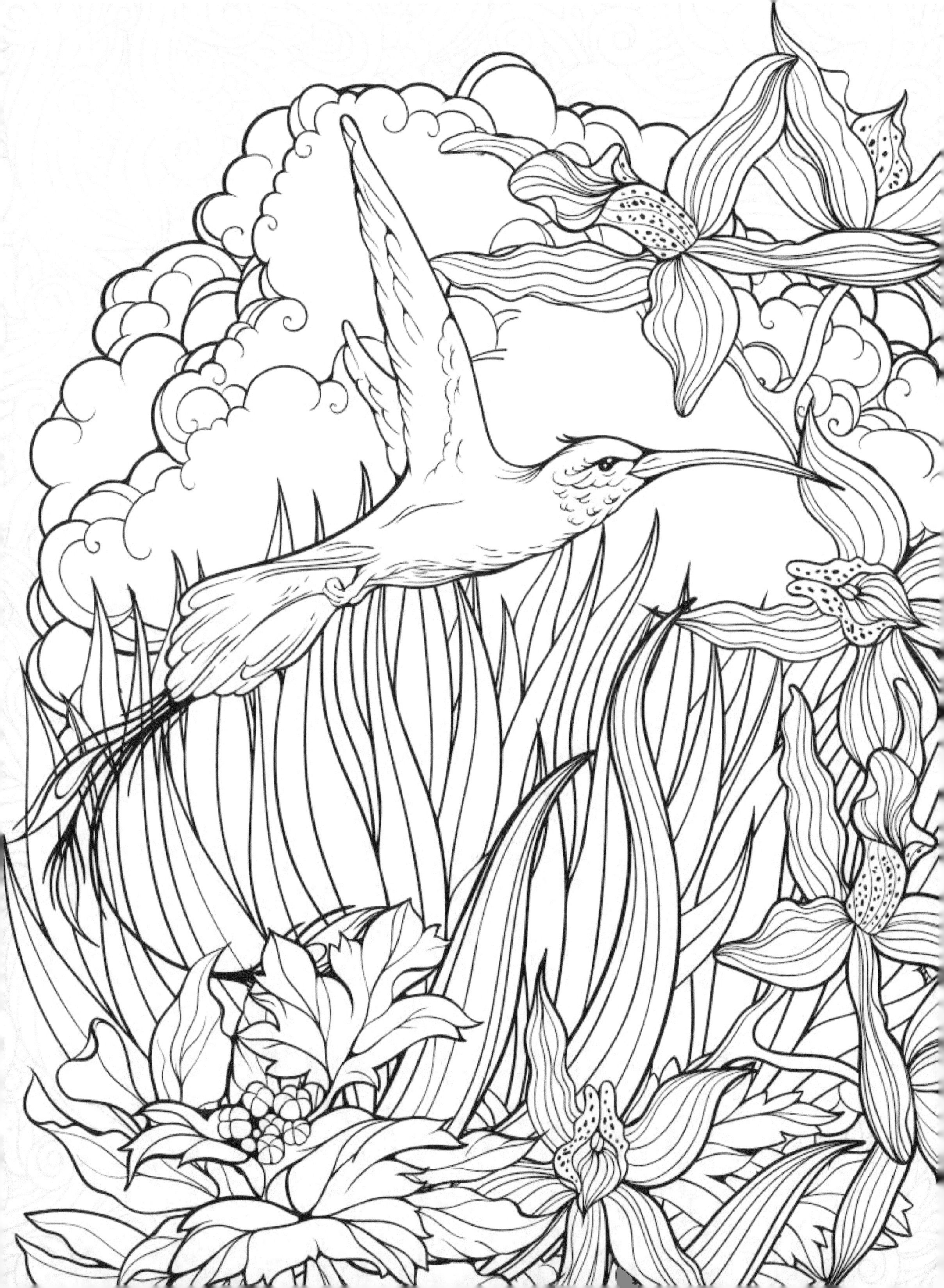

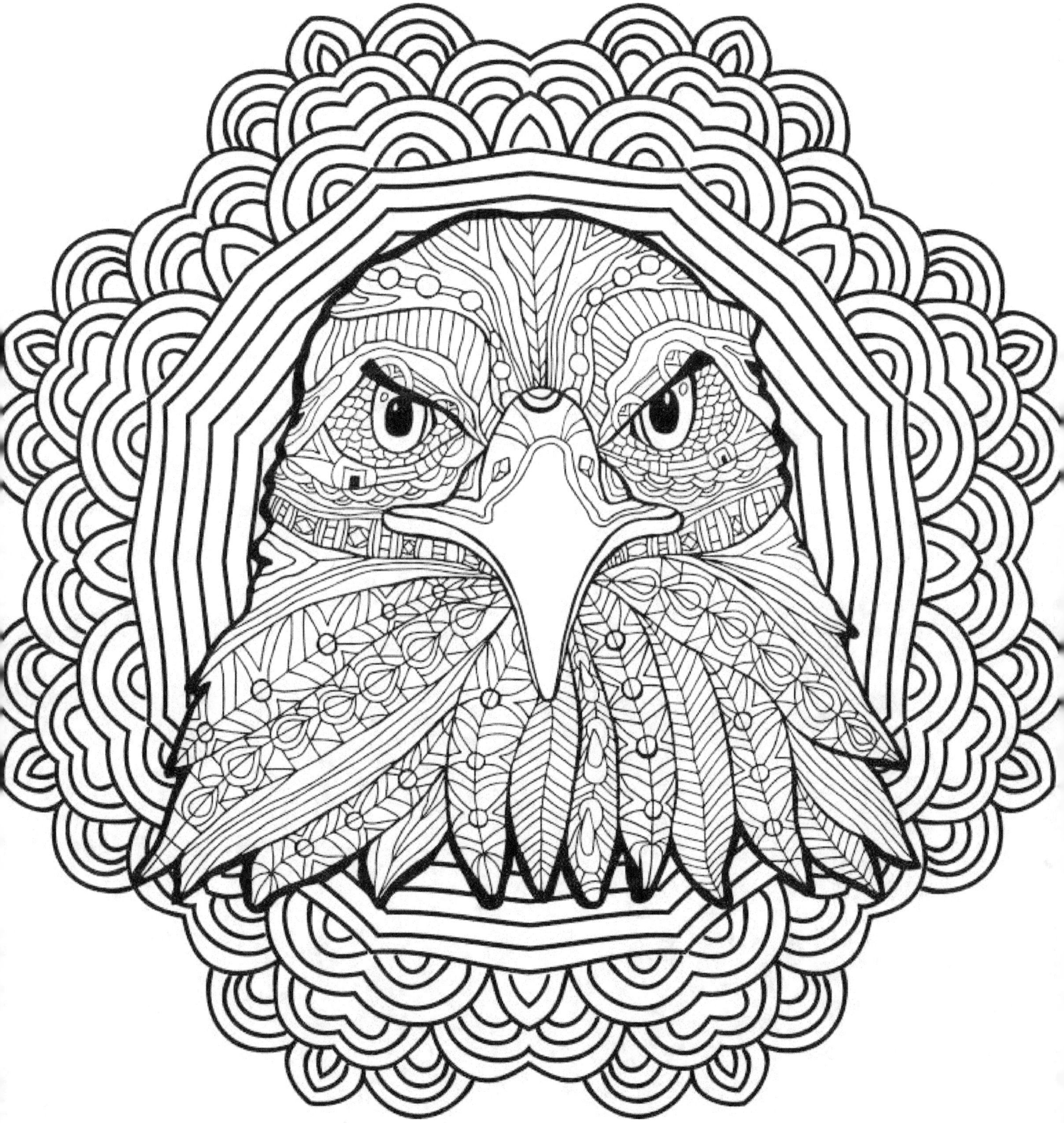

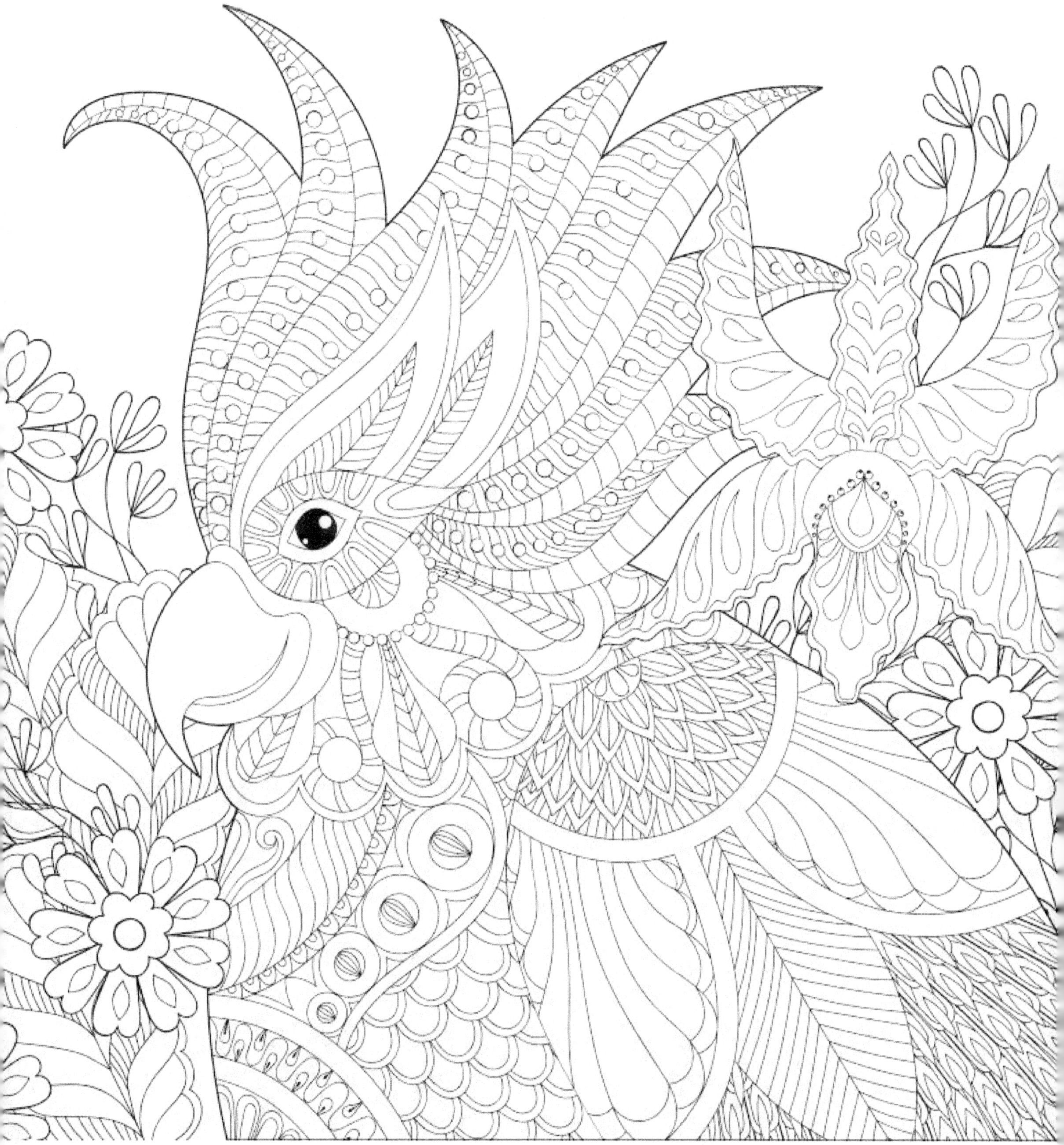

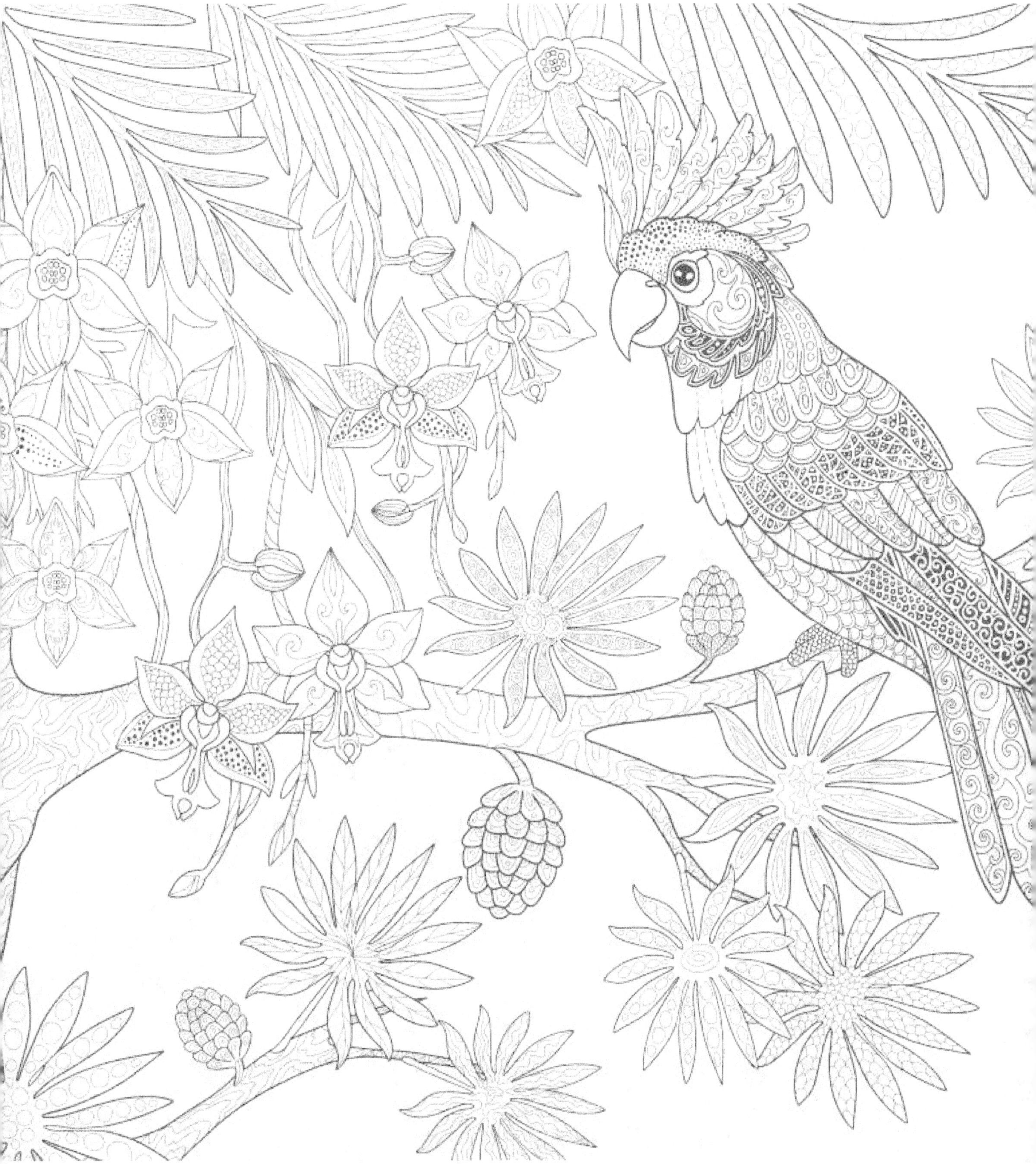

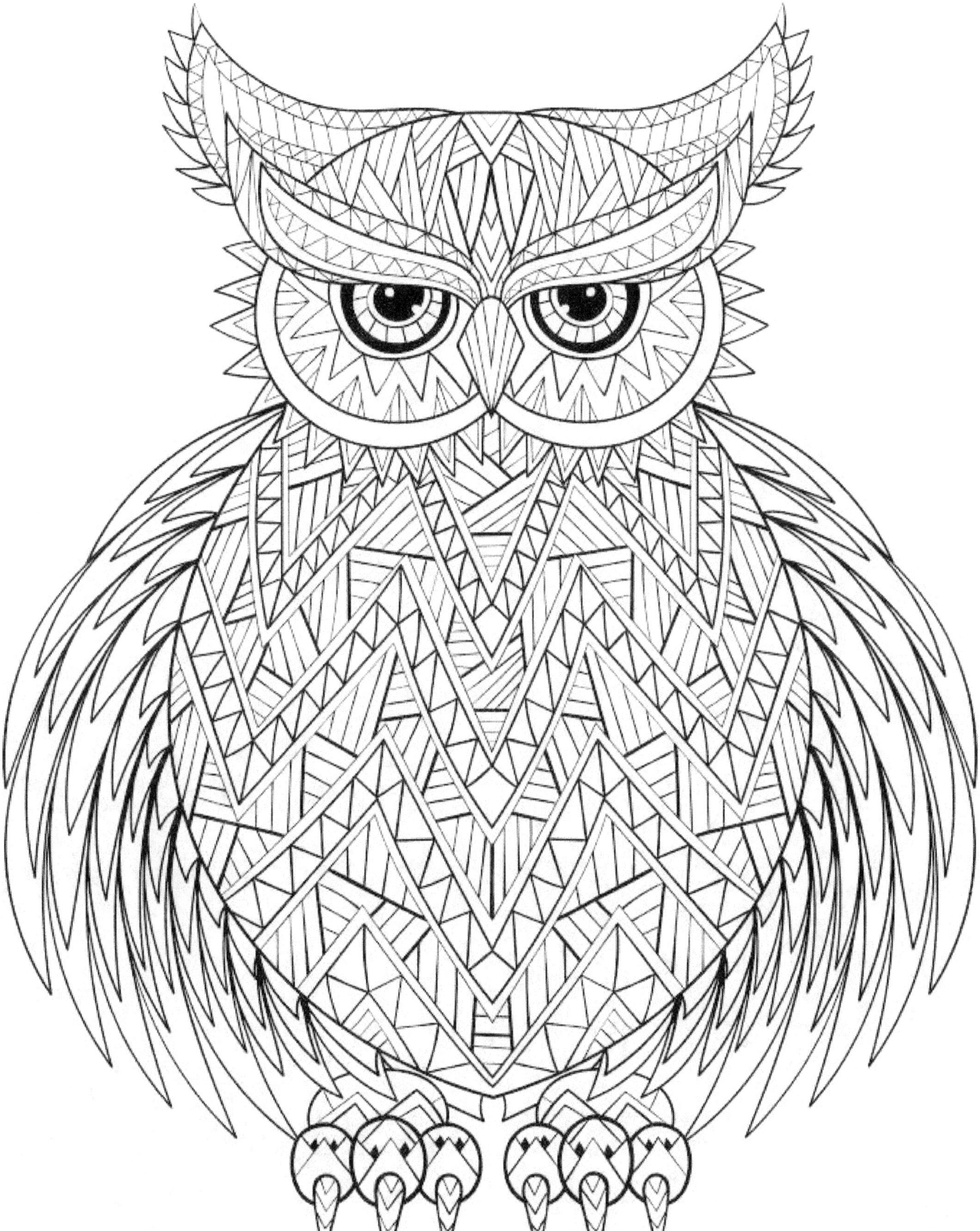

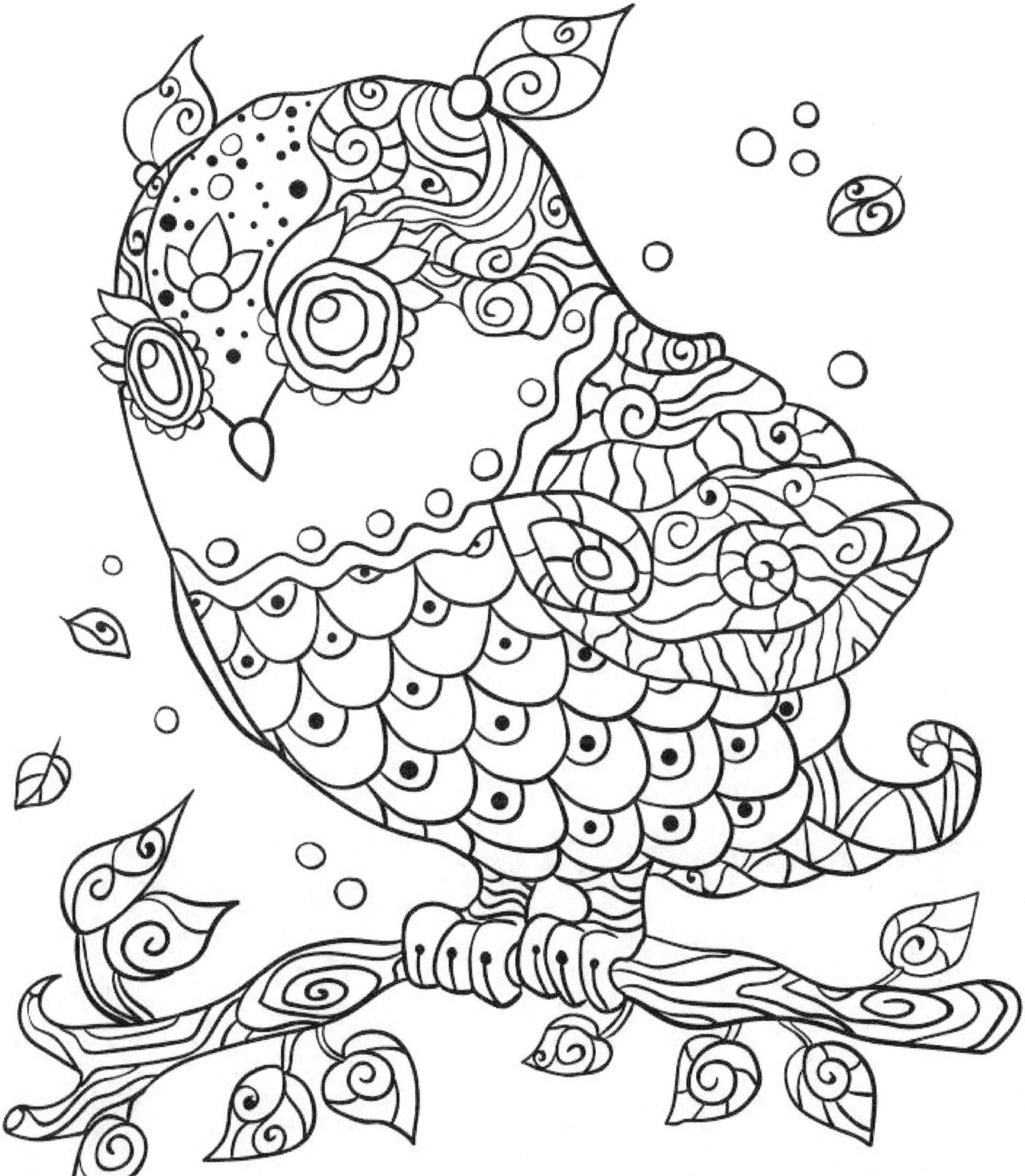

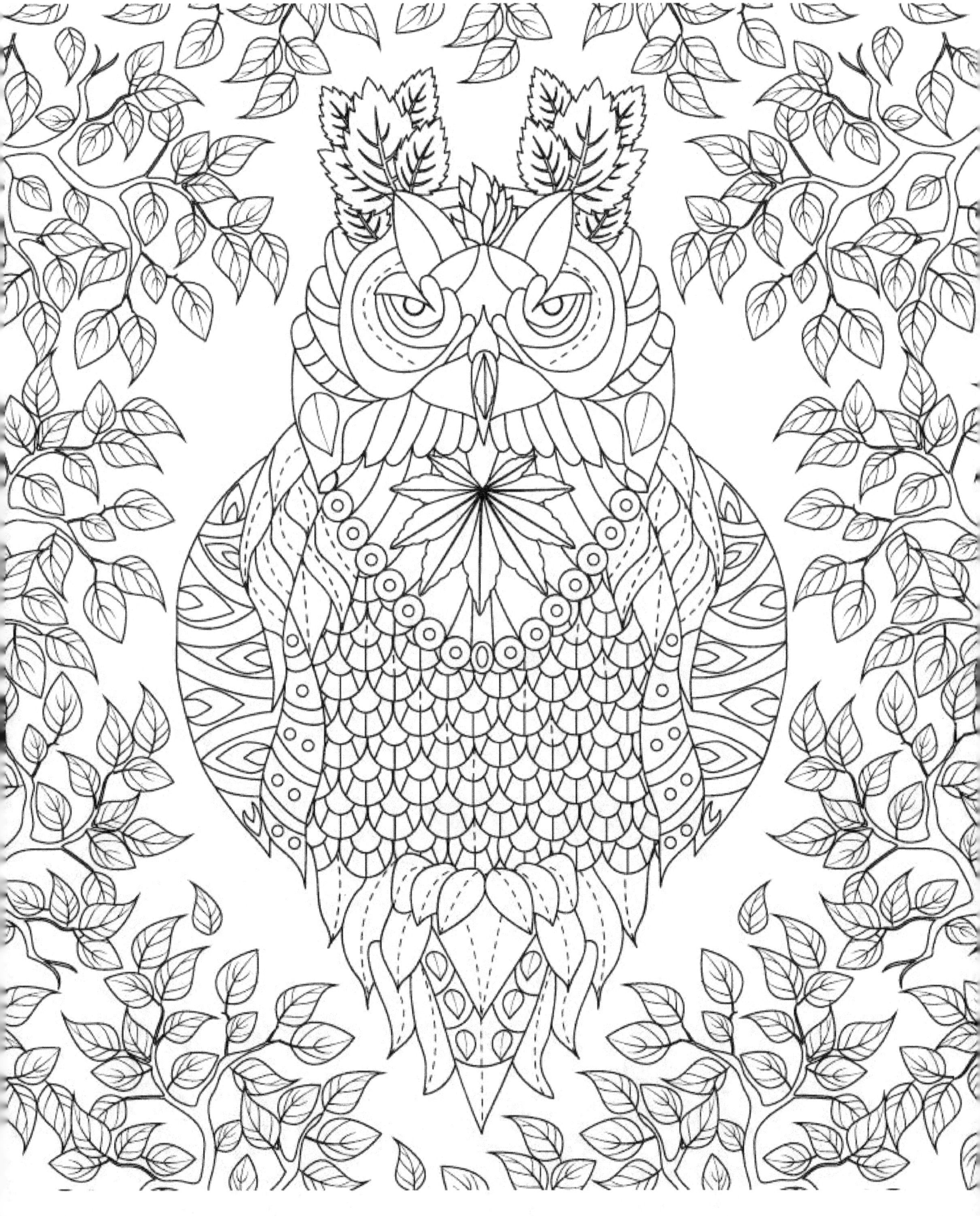

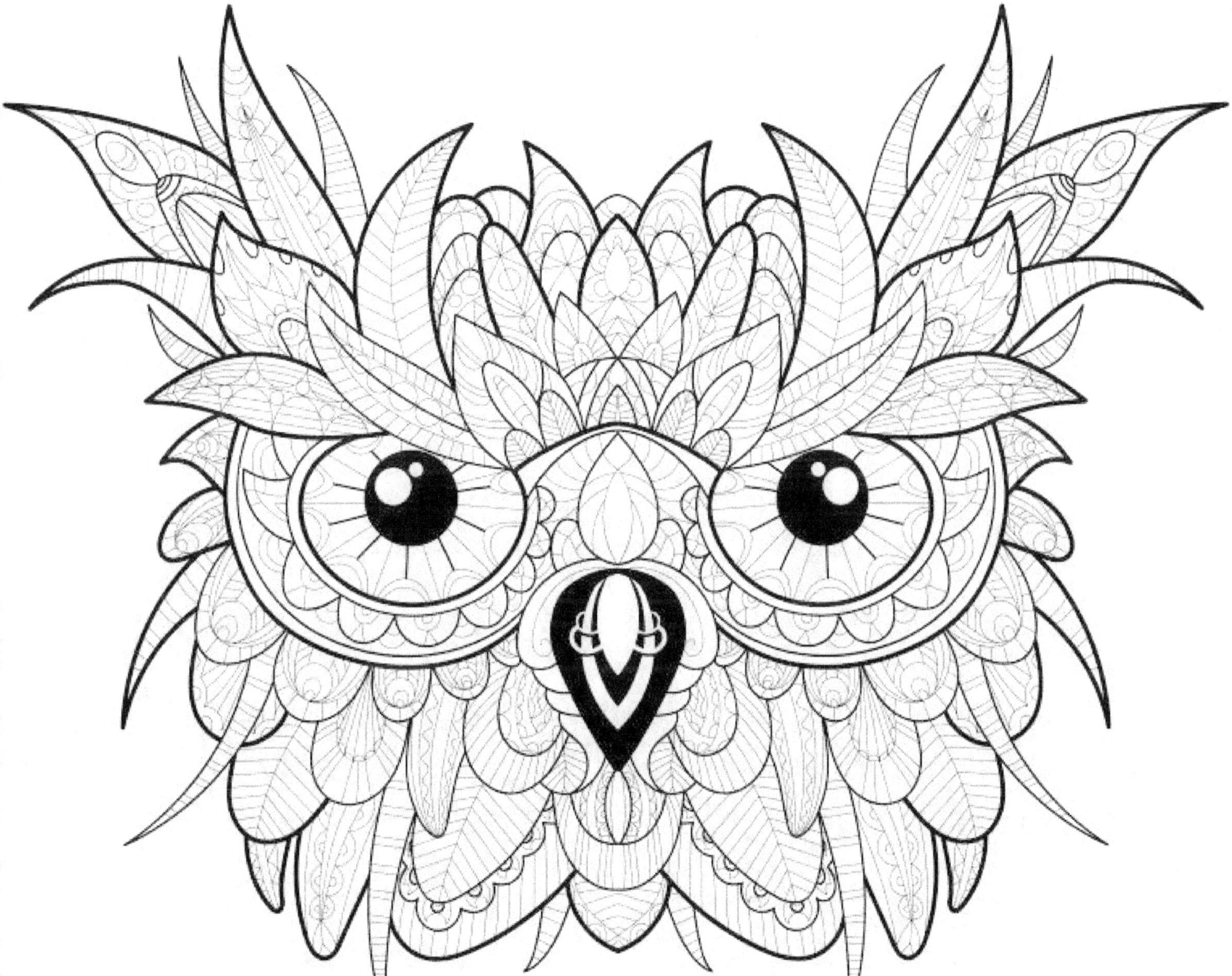

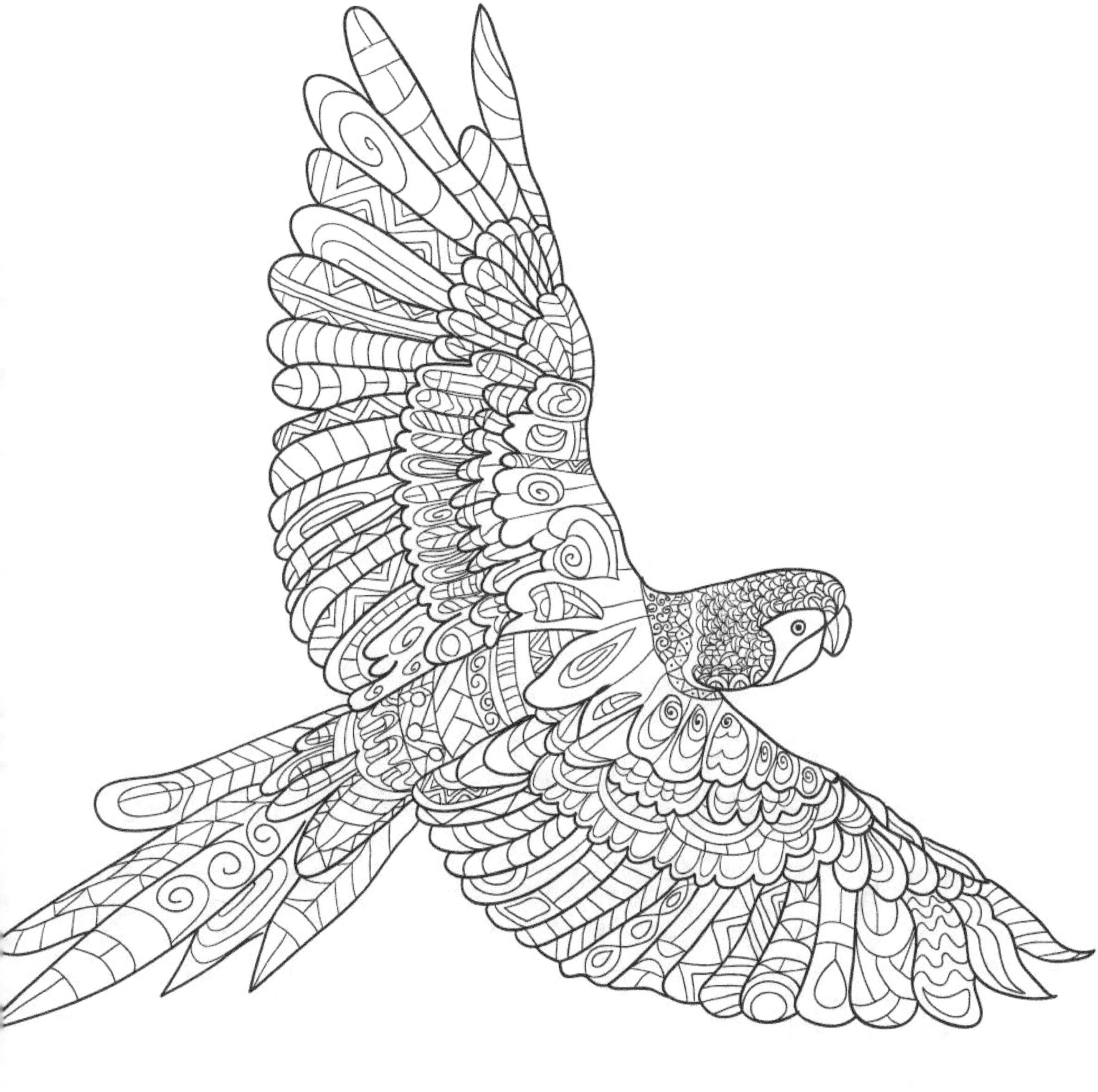

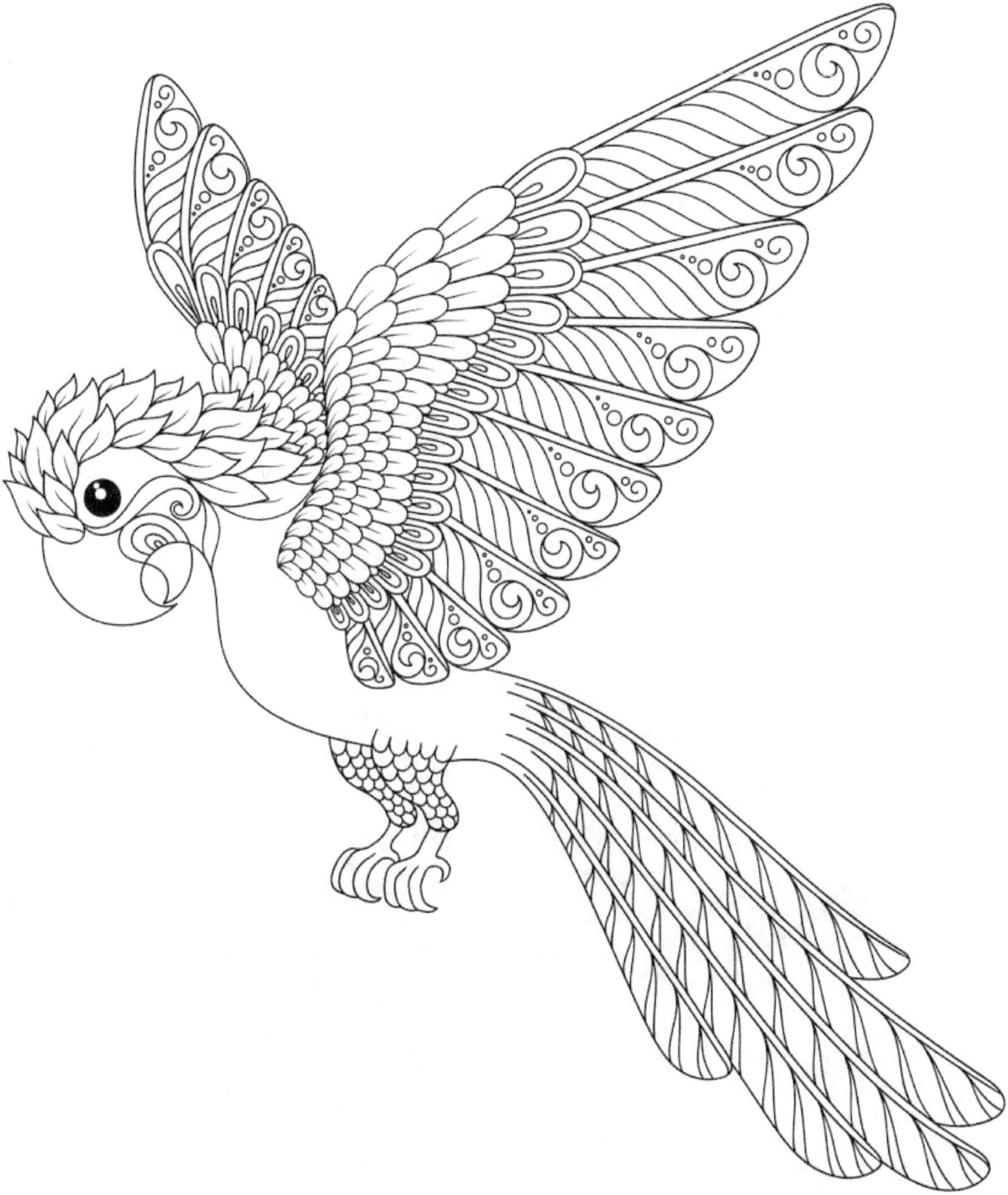

www.ingramcontent.com/pod-product-compliance
Lightning Source LLC
Chambersburg PA
CBHW081228170526
45165CB00009B/2993
9781547293162